Greetings f

THE NOR
WALES COAST

A VIEW OF THE NORTH WALES COAST
IN OLD PHOTOGRAPHS
AND PICTURE POSTCARDS

Cliff Hayes

PRINTWISE PUBLICATIONS LIMITED
1992

Published by Printwise Publications Ltd
47 Bradshaw Road, Tottington, Bury,
Lancs, BL8 3PW.

Warehouse and Orders
40-42 Willan Industrial Estate, Vere Street,
(off Eccles New Road),
Salford, M5 2GR.
Tel: 061-745 9168
Fax: 061-737 1755

ISBN No. 1 872226 44 2

Series editor

Printed and bound by Manchester Free Press, Paragon Mill, Jersey Street,
Manchester M4 6FP. Tel 061-236 8822.

FRONT COVER PICTURES:

Top Left: *The West Parade, Rhyl*
Bottom Left: *Rhydybenllig Bridge near Criccieth*
Top Right: *The Paddling Pool and Pavilion, Rhyl*
Bottom Right: *Gwrych Castle, Abergele*
Centre: *Promenade and Penmaen Head, Old Colwyn.*

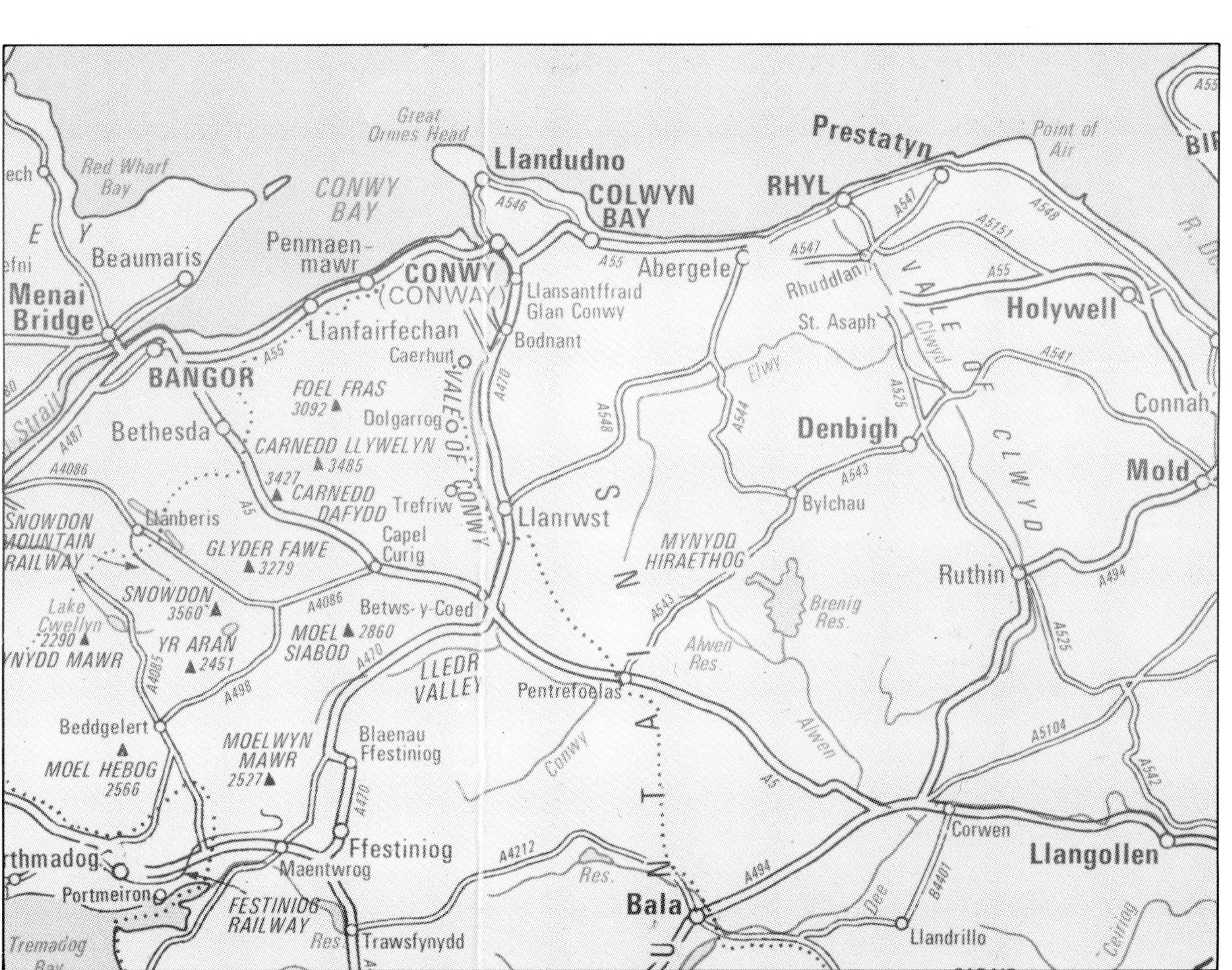

Great Ormes Head
Llandudno
Prestatyn
Point of Air
Red Wharf Bay
CONWY BAY
COLWYN BAY
RHYL
Beaumaris
Penmaen-mawr
CONWY (CONWAY)
Abergele
Rhuddlan
Holywell
Menai Bridge
Llansantffraid Glan Conwy
St. Asaph
Llanfairfechan
Bodnant
BANGOR
Caerhun
FOEL FRAS 3092
Dolgarrog
VALE OF CONWY
VALE OF CLWYD
Connah'
Bethesda
CARNEDD LLYWELYN 3485
Denbigh
Mold
3427 CARNEDD DAFYDD
Trefriw
Llanrwst
Bylchau
SNOWDON MOUNTAIN RAILWAY
Llanberis
Capel Curig
GLYDER FAWE 3279
MYNYDD HIRAETHOG
Ruthin
SNOWDON 3560
Betws-y-Coed
Lake Cwellyn
2290
MOEL SIABOD 2860
Brenig Res.
YR ARAN 2451
LLEDR VALLEY
Alwen Res.
Pentrefoelas
Beddgelert
Blaenau Ffestiniog
MOELWYN MAWR 2527
MOEL HEBOG 2566
Conwy
Alwen
Corwen
Ffestiniog
Llangollen
Maentwrog
Portmeiron
FESTINIOG RAILWAY
Res.
Bala
Trawsfynydd
Llandrillo
Tremadog Bay
Dee
Elwy
Clwyd
A55
A546
A547
A548
A5151
A541
A470
A543
A544
A525
A5
A4086
A487
A498
A4085
A494
A5104
A542
A4212
B4401

ABOUT THE AUTHOR

Born 1945 and brought up in The Ball O'Ditton, Widnes, when it was proper and part of Lancashire. Educated at Chestnut Lodge Infants, Simms Cross Junior and then Wade Deacon Grammar School in Widnes I then spent 4 years going to night school at The College of Art in Liverpool to study printing, Design and English.

From the age of 13 I have been involved in printing, working part-time at a small local printers, then getting an apprenticeship at Swale Press (Widnes Weekly News, Runcorn, Liverpool etc.) then started helping and writing for Mersey Beat and also writing a disc and pop column for the Weekly News.

Letchworth; Tinlings, Prescott: Ship's printer, Canadian Pacific to Canada and Cruising, Shaw Saville on Round the world trips and Japanese/Australian cruising etc; Book production in Blackpool; newspaper works manager in the Isle of Man; lino operator on National Newspapers (The Daily Mirror, The Sporting Chronicle, The Daily Telegraph etc); computer training and 12 months as print salesman all added to a broad view of every aspect of printing and of life in general.

Now settled in Manchester for the last 20 years and happily married with a teenage daughter. This is the eighth book I have had a hand in producing, but the first I have actually written from start to finish.

The author aged 3, carrying out early research in Rhyl.

INTRODUCTION

This book is the product of a real love affair between my family and the area referred to as North Wales. As part Liverpudlian, North Wales has always been the place to go. I have followed my family in heading for that beautiful area whenever the calendar got round to March, and rain or shine the rest of the year, most of our relaxation was done in this area. I now have an Uncle and Auntie in Rhos-on-Sea and cousins in chalets and caravans all over the coast.

Over the past 20 years my family and I have holidayed, week-ended and day-tripped into the area we respect and like so much.

So may we present to you a nostalgic look back at the area that has given millions of mortals so much pleasure, the area that is so tranquil yet so alive; the area that seems to say welcome to every spectrum of the human race with open arms, yet keeps the quiet dignity of the mountains just behind the coast. A magnificent yet friendly country.

After a busy week when the pressure of work and the world are often bearing down hard, it is nice to get away to North Wales and relax. To go for long walks along the beach, or a ramble in the country-side, visit a castle, or go and get a trout from the trout farm for tea. Sometimes we do nothing but sit, and enjoy the peace.

THANK YOU, NORTH WALES.

DIOLCH CYMRU

DEDICATION

This book is dedicated to all our friends at Presthaven, especially Ann & Tom Brassington; Rose & John Murphy; Greg Tracey; Lynn and Joanne Gilmore.

A mention also must be recorded for Doris Gibbens, the club receptionist at Presthaven, who passed away just before Christmas 1991. A more patient and understanding woman you would have to go a long way to find. She would sit for hours and listen to endless tales from the holiday makers. Tragedies and trifles, wonderful reasons why someone with a four berth caravan definitely had to have sixteen passes to the club. And a very red faced fourteen year old trying to impress on her that he was all of 18 and went in Night Clubs all the time. I've seen her at the height of the season with a 20-yard queue in front of her all asking for passes, listening patiently while a quarrelling couple explained that they had separated only the week before and the ex-wife had turned up with her family and he had turned up with his and could they have 12 passes for a six-berth caravan as neither was going home. She had heard it all before, and was always fair, and always tried her best to ensure everyone got what they wanted in the end. Doris will be greatly missed.

ACKNOWLEDGEMENTS

I would like to thank the Bay Book Shop in Colwyn Bay for providing some of the cards and leaflets used; Brian Hurst from Collectables; the post-card shop in Rhos-on-Sea for all their cards; Mr. H.D. Forton from Culcheth for the supply of rare postcards and Maurice Gilmour in Manchester Corn Exchange for his help.

WELCOME TO WALES

CROESO I GYMRU

ABERGELE

Bridge Street around 1900. Abergele is 5 miles west of Rhyl and only 1 mile inland. A lot off the pressure has been taken of the town since the new A55 motorway opened. I like calling in at Abergele early on a Sunday morning and visiting my mate Scotty and his book stall on the Sunday Market there every week. The large cattle market held on the third Wednesday of each month is an old institution in Abergele.

St. Michael's Church, Abergele in an early postcard from 1910 published by local Chemist: F.J. Boardman. The Church was restored in 1879 but the chancel dates back to 1511, part of the church was once used as the village school. Records show that one of the gravestones in this old church says that a man lived three miles north of the church. Today this would be nearly 2 miles out at sea. Also we know that in 1778 Thomas Pennant (the Welsh naturalist) wrote that walking on the beach at low tide he ''saw a bank of loam and soil out at sea and on it were the stumps of oak trees in a good state of preservation but soft as wax when touched''. The coast must have gone out much further, and the landscape very different in the 1600's than it is today.

IN THE MIDST OF LIFE WE ARE IN DEATH

The Monument, Abergele Churchyard.

Two local disaster are commemorated in this fine monument in Abergele Churchyard. The wrecking of the Ocean Monarch in 1884 and the crash of the Irish Mail Train in Pensarn in 1868.

BALA (Y BALA)

It's a lovely run from Llangollen down through Corwen and then on the back road to Bala, bringing you out at the lake side at the northern terminal of the Bala Lake Railway. In steam train days the train journey from Llangollen to the back of Bala Lake then on to Barmouth must have been one of the most picturesque in Great Britain. The stretch down the back of Bala Lake has been relayed as a narrow gauge steam railway and is a real treat to travel on.

You pass through Carrog on that recommended run from Llangollen. A timeless view of the river Dee wandering down to the sea. Very hard to date, this Frith's postcard is actually from the 1950s.

This card clearly says 'Horse Shoe Pass near Bala', but I would have put it down as near Llangollen. Dated about 1920 it must have been hair-raising to negotiate the pass in early motoring days.

Horse Shoe Pass near Bala.

A1783. THE LAKE AND ARRAN MOUNTAIN, BALA.

The Lake and Arran Mountain, Bala. This painting rather than photograph shows the lake and the mixture of peace and splendour at Bala. A great stopping place on trips to Wales. (A pat on the back for Bala, the toilets and facilities at the north of the town are always open and clean).

BALA

A general view of Bala with the lake behind in this 1940 card from Valentine's.

This card shows Bala High Street sometime between the wars. Try and be more exact with the dates by using the cars as guides.

BANGOR

Bangor is often missed by visitors as people head across the Menai Straights and into Anglesey. Said to be one of the oldest towns in Wales, Bangor dates from around 525 A.D. Its name comes from Ban-Chor meaning High Choir and is connected with the monastry founded there by Deiniol. Bangor Cathedral is originally Norman, and has been much rebuilt and restored throughout time. Unfortunately it is in a dip, so it presents no grand outline or view, but is well worth a visit. These two views from 1895.

Postcard Publishers have put the longest name in Wales on everything. Here is a view of the Menai Bridge and Old Bangor but labelled with Llanfair etc. gogogoch. The bridge was built by Thomas Telford in 1819-26. When it first opened this bridge had the longest single span in the world, and the Admiralty had demanded 100ft headroom.

The Britannia Railway Bridge built by Robert Stephenson in 1846-50 to carry Holyhead-London expresses over the Menai Strait at a height of 200ft. The twin tracks were enclosed in wooden tubes but these were damaged by fire in 1970 and have now been replaced by open steelwork. The bridge now carries a new road linking Anglesey to the mainland. Note the giant lions at each end of the bridge.

BETWS-Y-COED

The Chapel-in-the-Wood. This natural cross-roads seems best known for the Swallow Falls today. But in the 1920s and 1930s it was famous for trout and even salmon fishing and its lovely Fairy Glen.

The Conway Falls Cafe in Betws-y-coed. Another example of a postcard's long life, this card was printed before 1920 but not posted till 1930s (10 years later).

This artist's impression of the falls in a series from Valentine & Sons shows the splendour that has drawn millions to Betws-y-coed. Note the spelling with 2 t's. It was spelt with 2 t's until the 1920s when it was proved that there were no double t's in Welsh and many names were altered. This helps date the post card.

Again the double 't' dates this card before the 1920s. There is something about the water rushing over the falls that draws people.

The Fairy Glen and the 'Enchanted Pool of Reflection'

Another fine view of the Fairy Glen, this one was a very popular postcard at the turn of the century and sold for many, many years.

On the Llugwy-Old Bridge above the Swallow Falls, Bettws-y-Coed (from Oil Painting by W.H. Mander).

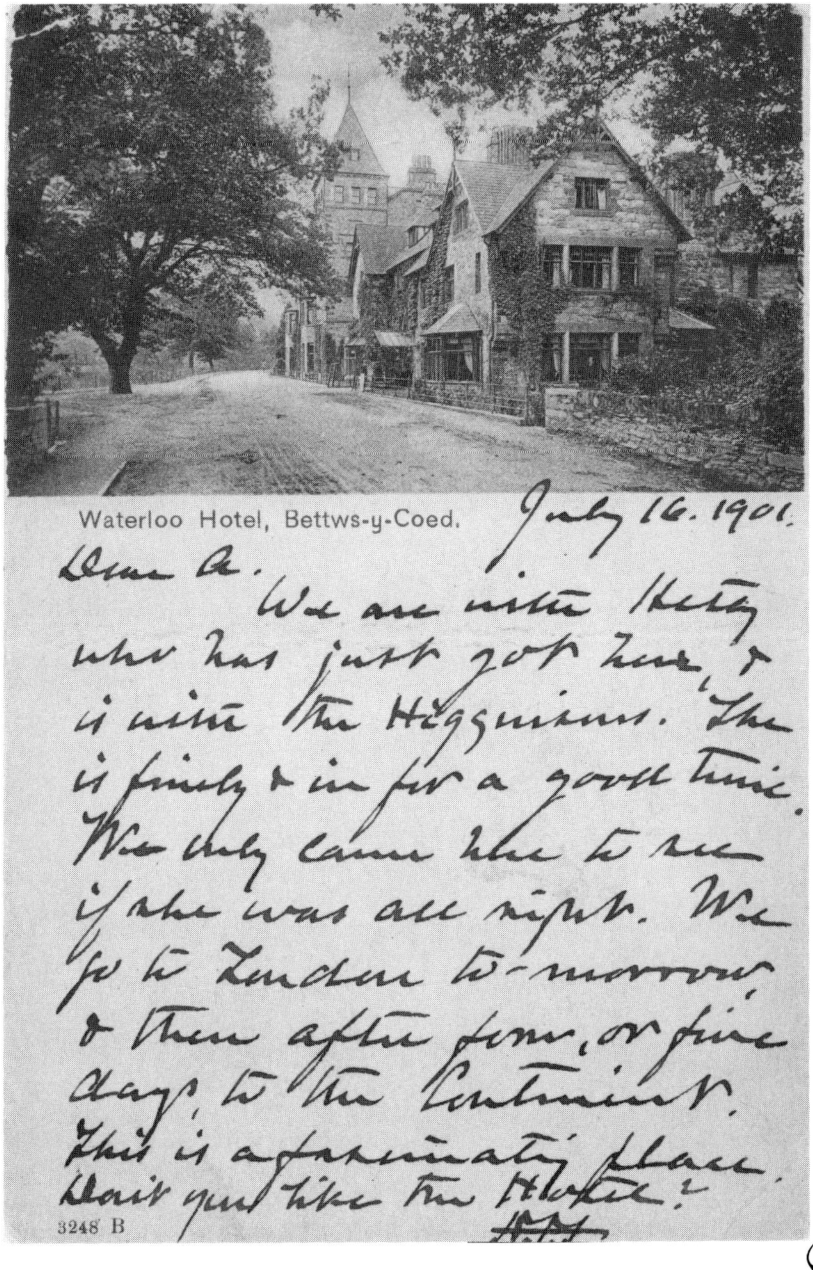

Waterloo Hotel, Bettws-y-Coed.

July 16. 1901.

Dear A.

We are with Hetty who has just got here, & is with the Higginsons. She is finely & in for a good time. We only came here to see if she was all right. We go to London to-morrow, & then after four or five days to the Continent. This is a fascinating place. Don't you like the Hotel?

A.M.

3248 B

The Waterloo Hotel, Betws-y-Coed kindly dated by A.M. the writer as July 16, 1901. The hotel is still there and still recognisable. What an adventure lay ahead for them, London tomorrow, then after 4 or 5 days on to the continent, she writes, and all starting in Betws-y-Coed.

Note: I'm constantly amazed at the simplicity of the addresses on old postcards. This one states Miss Ada Bouve, Kingham, Mass. U.S.A., and presumably it got there and then found it's way back to me.

BODELWYDDAN
(MARBLE) CHURCH.
A.1776.

BODELWYDDAN

The Marble Church and its 202ft spire built by Dowager Lady Willoughby de Broke as a memorial to her husband. This lovely church was always something to look out for on the coach trip to Llandudno or Colwyn Bay. The grave yard shows its fascinating connection with Canada and a military camp at the end of the First World War, with the graves of the young Canadian servicemen. Alan Bleasdale told the story in 'Monocled Mutineer'. The church was built around 1860 at a cost of £60,000.

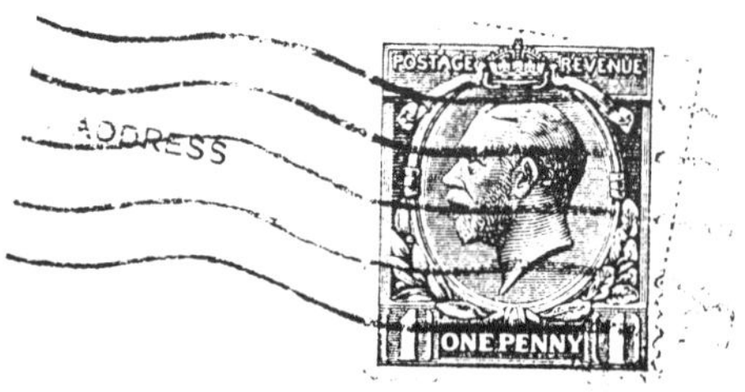

BODNANT HALL

Bodnant Gardens are famous and visited by thousands each year. But this is the Hall about 1912. Again a story of sorts on the back. The card was posted in 1917 but it was published by R. Richards, Talycafn and printed in Germany. As no printing went to Germany after 1914 because of the War it must have been printed before. It is a wonder that 'Printed in Germany' wasn't crossed off or the cards withdrawn as anti-German feelings were high when it was posted.

CAERNARVON (CAERNARFON)

Caernarvon is in command of the southern end of the Menai Straits with the castle built around 1283. Edward II was born in the town on 25th April 1284, though where he was born is much debated. 'Caer-ar-Fon' or 'Fortress facing Anglesey' is a very ancient place, Cear Seiont was the old British name and Segontium the Roman name and the river there bears the old name Seiont.

Again spelling helps date these postcards. CAR at the start of Caernarvon dates them before the First World War. The present CAER was not used until after 1918. A card showing no E on the face and an E on the back denotes it is a reprint.

CARNARVON CASTLE.

06107

Both cards date from around 1912.

Maypole shops were once familiar all over North Wales but this shop is definitely in Caernarfon and taken in 1902.

Siop groser y' Maypole' yng Nghaerfon.

COLWYN BAY (BAE COLWYN)

What we now refer to as Colwyn Bay only grew up at the turn of the century. In 1866 there was only one building Pwll-y-Crochan Hall and what was Colwyn then is now Old Colwyn. Colwyn Bay got its name from Mr Porter the owner of the hotel that was converted from Pwll-y-Crochan Hall.

When a youngster and teenager I always seemed to miss Colwyn Bay, either stopping before at Rhyl or feeling brave going on to Llandudno. Nowadays I enjoy Colwyn Bay. The second-hand book shop there is great for browsing, and the Crown Hotel is ideal to pop in for a meal. Pop into the W.H. Smith's in the main street, the Victorian verandah outside so well preserved, and inside too the plaster and ceiling are beautiful. It is a very friendly little town. The main road even sinks out of sight by the station to leave Colwyn Bay in peace as the A55 speeds on. But it is well worth turning off for, there is Welsh Mountain Zoo and the unusual restaurant at the station (Platform 5).

Colwyn Bay from the Woods 1895.

COLWYN BAY

Colwyn Bay was very high in the entertainment stakes in the early 1900s. Built into the embankment this theatre had to stop every time a train went through because the audience could not hear the artists.

Yet another Llanfairgogogogoch used out of context. Two good views of Colwyn Bay in 1910 Denis postcard.

A fine view of the pier, crowded and bustling. Going past today and seeing it boarded and shut up seems such a waste.

COLWYN BAY

Sent to Mr & Mrs Isles the Fruitiers in Mostyn Lane, Chain Bar, Failsworth, Manchester and posted at 9.15 on April 14th 1925. It claimed good weather and enjoyment at this resort.

The countryside of Colwyn Bay in this 1909 card from Valentines' Phototone Series shows the Dingle Bridge in the Pwyllycrochan Woods behind Colyn Bay.

THE PIER

BEACH PONIES

THE PROMENADE & PENMAENHEAD

COLWYN BAY

THE CHALETS, PROMENADE & PIER

MINIATURE RAILWAY & PROMENADE

Colwyn Bay, showing a rare view of the miniature railway (bottom right) dated about 1928-30? Composite cards have a peculiarity about them; while some cards show 4 or 5 scenes taken by the same person at the same time, others were put together from whatever was on file, and can feature shots taken up to 10 years apart on one composite card.

COLWYN BAY

This card is earlier and shows how popular walking in Eirias Park and The Dingle was.

LIVERPOOL & NORTH WALES

EASTER SAILINGS (Good Friday to Easter Monday)
DAILY, Whitsuntide to 23rd September, 1935.

Turbine Steamer " ST. TUDNO " or " ST. SEIRIOL."
Leaves Liverpool **10.45** a.m. for Llandudno (four hours ashore) and Menai Bridge (one hour ashore), weather, etc., permitting. Due back **7.30** p.m. Bangor or Beaumaris Passengers with Single or Period Tickets proceed from Menai Bridge (Free Bus conveyance).

Return Day Fare from Liverpool to Llandudno 6/-, 1st Class 8/-
" " " " Menai Bridge 8/-, 1st Class 10/-
Half-day Sailings certain Wednesdays, Saturdays and Sundays.
Through Bookings from Principal Railway Stations, also Interchange Rail and Boat Tickets.
Special Boat Fares for Parties of eight or more, including **Free Pass** for Promoter of Parties exceeding 25 in number.

Frequent Day Trips from Liverpool.
Round the Island of Anglesey—170 miles sail. (*See Bills.*)
Daily from Llandudno at **1.15** p.m. to Menai Bridge, and on certain Tuesdays to Douglas. Also Frequent Excursions Round the Island of Anglesey. (*See Bills.*)

Excellent Catering on Board.
Contracts from **21**/- Official Guide **2d.** Post Free.
For conditions of carriage and all further particulars apply to the Liverpool and North Wales Steamship Company Limited, 40, Chapel Street, Liverpool.
'Phone, Central **1654.** T. G. Brew, Secretary.

From a Dennis Composite Card from 1960. A bright shot of the Welsh Mountain Zoo above Colwyn Bay. Well worth pulling off the A55 and visiting.

1955 and a much more crowded Colwyn Bay. Now that the motorways and coast road are open I can see North Wales becoming a commuter belt for Liverpool and Manchester. It's very sad but probably true.

CONWAY (CONWY)

Now as you speed under the river at Conway spare a thought for the millions who queued for 3 and 4 hours to cross the river. Just imagine when there was only one bridge. Conway, the name is derived from Cyn-wy (principal river) was always an important military town. The huddle of houses dominated by the castle has always attracted visitors.

An aerial view of the three bridges that now span the river. The Suspension Bridge, opened in 1826 is similar in design to that of the Menai Bridge. It was begun in 1822, after a disaster to the ferry boat that was the only means of crossing, caused the loss of the 13 lives. The Government at the time promised a safer crossing and the bridge was started. It was replaced in 1959 by a new road bridge, and it is now preserved by the National Trust for pedestrians only. Another crossing was opened in 1991 by Her Majesty the Queen, a tunnel to help ease the congestion and long traffic jams so long associated with the town.

CONWAY

Conway Castle and Bridge. This view must be one of the most photographed or painted views in Wales. The top card is from September 1931 and the one below an earlier one from 1910. That's when they were posted, the dating of the actual taking of the photo is harder, the lack of people and cars leave the ivy and that boat as your only clues.

A very pleasant, if a bit stark, view of the river mouth with the Castle and Bridge in the foreground and the Orme on the skyline. A Valentine "Silveresque" card from the late 1940s.

Many many different cards have been issued in connection with the smallest house in Great Britain. This one from 1912 is a very local affair published by Mrs. E. Williams, 11 Lowergate Street, Conway and printed in the town, it shows the inside of the house.

DYSERTH WATERFALL. A.1775.

DYSERTH

The 40ft waterfall at Dyserth has always been the main attraction there and it was always included, and still is, in tours from Prestatyn and Rhyl. In Victorian times the tea-rooms and entertainments made it a very pleasant afternoon. The pubs in and around the village are still worth a visit. Dyserth also boasts an old church with a 'Jesse' window, said to have come from Basingwerk Abbey, and a well flattened and razed to the ground castle that Llewellyn-y-Gryffyed took apart in 1260. Dyserth was even mentioned in that oft-quoted volume, The Domesday Book, spelt Dissart it boasted a church, a priest and a mill.

A good view from about 1928 showing the extensive gardens at the foot of the falls. The writer had just paid 6d for a lovely afternoon and was informing her mum back in Fairview, Bacup, Lancs.

An idyllic scene of a gentle, restful lane leading to the shore, about 1935.

GRONANT

Gronant, once called Upper Gronant, is a smallish place and a nice quiet backwater, mostly overlooked. Lower Gronant, which consists of Shore Road, and Presthaven Sands Camp and other caravan camps, together with some shops and the Beachcomber Pub where they serve some of the cheapest good value lunches in the area. A family can enjoy a full Sunday lunch, and a drink for under £10.

Below: The Abbey was a retreat and a place of pilgrimage. Now it looks like ending up as a hotel. The Abbey bell was rung day and night (as anyone who had a caravan in the area will testify).

Above: There was a subtle switch from coming to Wales and going out every day to somewhere different that was so much in vogue in the early 1900s to getting to your holiday destination and not moving at all until you went home. I think this card is from about 1938 and the stay-put brigade are growing, along with the caravans and pre-fabs on the other side of the dunes.

During the First World War the area from Lower Gronant to Talacre contained a large Army Camp. It was here that the Canadians and some Americans waited to travel to Liverpool to be shipped home after the war. Rumours and delays led to a mutiny and riots, and some men were shot. The area is a fascinating mishmash of modern sleek caravans, and camps and caravans that are really homely and lived in. From modern purpose built bungalows to well loved prefabs that look as if they could collapse in the strong Talacre wind.

This 1938 combination shows (A) the build up of caravans, although the best laid out site seems to be inland of the railway.
(B) The drainage from Prestatyn and the lock gate made the Warren Bridge, which is still a pleasant walk today.
(C) What a mixture of corrugation and caravan. Those were the days.
(D) Gronant Drug Store — everything for the early camper.
(E) Upper Gronant has not changed much and the Gronant Arms right is still there and serving a nice pint.

Taken from the top of the sandhills. What memories of early self catering this postcard invokes. Today you would not entertain any of these huts or vans, but in 1938 visitors sent home this view with pride. Many of these cards are marked with arrows and "we are here" as Scousers, Brummies and Mancunians descended on the coast to enjoy a cheap holiday. The building on the right foreground is now the Anchorage Pub where we recently enjoyed a Golden Wedding celebration with our friends Anne and Tom.

Two advertisements from 1859. Note the names for the coaches, so much more exciting to take the Empress Coach than to catch the 2.30 bus.

Coach Tours in North Wales.

TO VISITORS AND OTHERS.

MR. C. A. HARTLEY'S COACHES,

"The Prince of Wales," "The Old Times," "The Wonder," and "The Empress," RUN DAILY (and several times a day on the short routes), to the most

Picturesque and Beautiful Parts of North Wales.

For Fares and Times of Starting, apply at the Booking Office,

QUEEN'S HOTEL GARDENS, Clonmel Street, LLANDUDNO.

LLANDUDNO.

GRIFFITHS'

Nottingham Restaurant and Boarding House,

15, LOWER MOSTYN STREET.

Breakfasts, Dinners and Teas . .

AT MODERATE CHARGES.

LARGE DINING ROOM.

PARTIES CATERED FOR.

ACCOMMODATION FOR CYCLISTS. WRITE FOR TERMS.

HOLYWELL (TREFFYNNON)

Holywell as the name suggests comes from the fact there is a Holy Well there. The story of St. Winifred is a little gruesome but for those who do not know it — Winifred, a fair Welsh maiden was loved by Caradoc a local Prince. She spurned his love as she was intent on becoming a Nun. Fleeing from his advances he drew his sword and chased her, somehow off came her head, and rolled down the hill to where her uncle St. Beuno was preaching in the local church. He picked up the head and placed it back on the body and miraculously the lady was restored whole. A well sprang up where her head rested and the earth opened and swallowed Prince Caradoc. The spring is in the crypt of St. Winifred's Chapel and on numerous visits we have made to the well the peace and tranquility of the place make it something very special. The waters there have never frozen and are thought to have restorative properties. Kings, Queens, and nobility, have all made pilgrimages, but there doesn't seem to be as many pilgrims today — pity.

St. Winifred's Bath. Note the handrails to help those swimming or emersing. The inner spring is through the arches behind.

A later card than the previous one, with the addition of the crucifix and screen on the crypt and the chandelier with lit candles above.

This card shows the small church and the building covering the Well in about 1948.

An early card from 1930 showing the Well House.

LLANDUDNO

'Queen of the North Wales Coast' she was crowned in the Victorian heyday and Queen Llandudno always will be. The town has always been that little bit harder to get to and therefore an exclusiveness and selectiveness seems to prevail. Many in the 1960s and 1970s seemed to set out for a day in Llandudno only to give up in traffic jams and spend the day elsewhere on the coast.

This photocrom card was taken in early 1950 though posted in August 1957. Some cards came out year after year. Happy Valley really was a place of great entertainment and a ''must'' for a visit. Mr and Mrs Powell write back to their neighbours in Spotland, Rochdale, saying ''the gales have blown all night and are still blowing strong'', luck of the draw with English holidays!

These two postcards are good examples of the chance and art of dating postcards. The top one is posted 1906, but the trees are fairly mature. The bottom one is posted four years later, 1910, but taken from almost the very same spot and the trees are definitely younger. Both are different card companies, the second is a Peacock Card.

Trees, mosses, ivy etc, can help date cards.

A 1906 card showing the bathing huts awaiting the turn of the tide. Note the trees on the promenade. (Kings Series, Llandudno).

LLANDUDNO

A Dennis card from the late 1940s shows a clean and tidy Llandudno with still lots of green fields on the far side of the bay and behind the promenade.

The minstrals in Happy Valley entertain the visitors. I hope you can see the lovely bonnets on the ladies in the bottom right corner. This card published by the West End Post Office owner Alec Taylor was dropped into the post box in 1918 only weeks after the end of the First World War. I wonder how Lucy felt writing how nice and peaceful a time she was having in Llandudno to her friend Edith Murshead in Moss Brook, Cheadle.

A 1906 card showing the beauty of the hills and mountains behind the town. Camera Hill was the name given to part of the Orme for a while in the early Edwardian period.

The bay has always been good for boats and boating. This 1905 card shows many small craft enjoying the shelter of the bay.

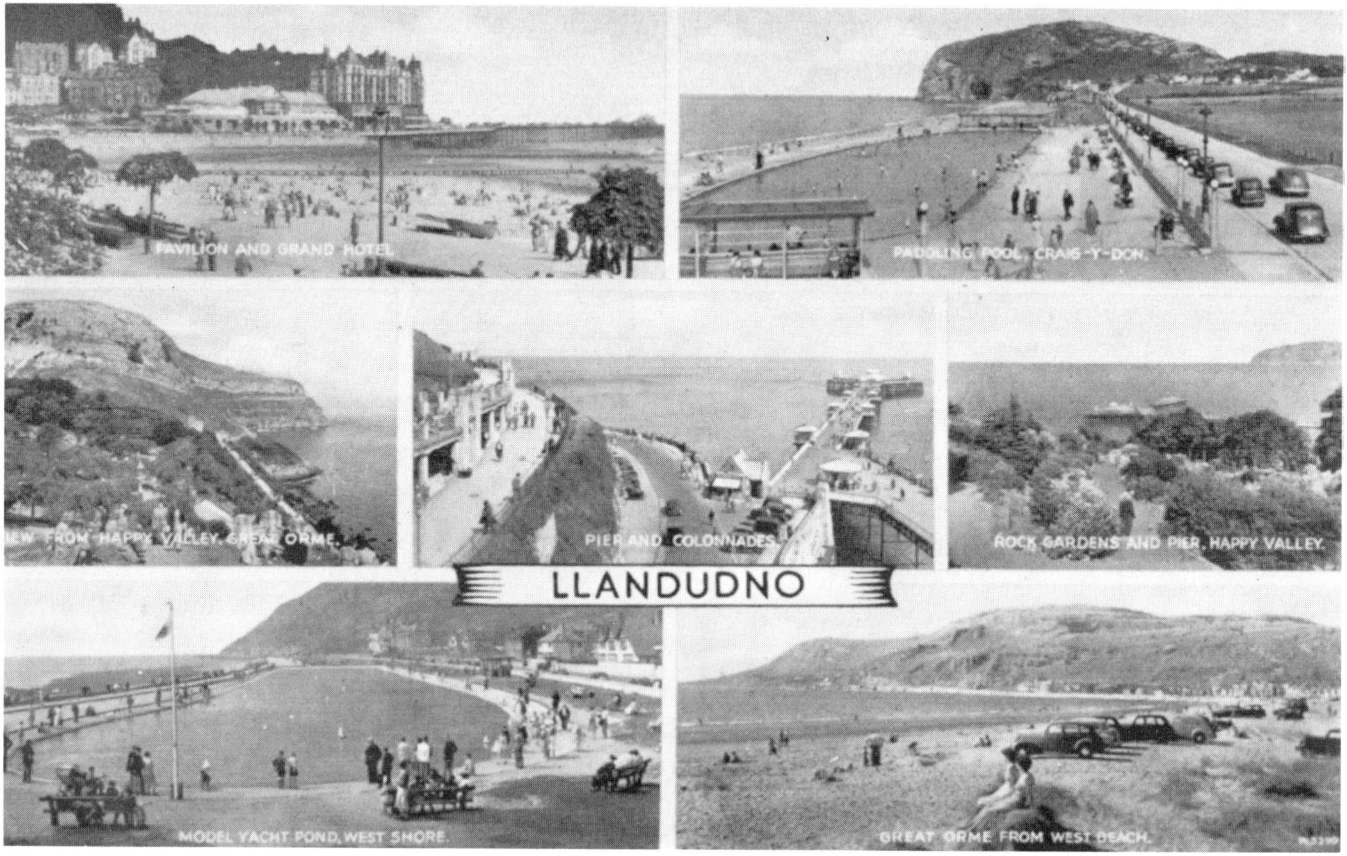

A very full collation from 1948 and the Valentine Card Company, shows three of the lesser known sides of Llandudno.

Look back a few pages and compare how built up the town has become behind the front row of the promenade. This Salmon card from the 1950s shows clearly the growth in houses in Llandudno.

An unusual and moody card from 1912. The west shore beech looking across the mouth of the river and down the coast. Complete solitude.

An advert from 1898

VINCENT'S

High-class Private and Family Hotel,

... Llandudno.

SITUATED in the centre of the **Marine Parade,** and possesses the most extensive sea frontage on the Parade; also an uninterrupted and commanding view of the Carnarvonshire Mountains.

Private Sitting Rooms facing the Sea.

LOFTY AND WELL-ARRANGED SMOKING AND BILLIARD ROOMS.

EXTENSIVE TENNIS COURTS.

TARIFF (graduated according to the season of the year) on application to

JOHN VINCENT, Proprietor.

It's interesting to read what was a draw and important in 1900. Smoking and Billiard rooms and tennis courts would not be high on the list of musts nowadays.

The following five pictures come from a booklet dated 1897 telling for 6d how healthy the North Wales coast is. Published by A.L. Allday of the Shakespeare Press they were very popular reading in winter for planning the coming holidays.

The Little Orme viewed from Llandudno and the one thing that strikes you immediately is the absence of houses. This picture from 1895.

The newly completed Pier Pavilion although the first part of what is termed the Pier really runs alongside the rock.

LLANDUDNO

The Baths Hotel — it claims on the side of the tall building in the middle of the photograph. Now the Grand Hotel.

A strangely simple and unadorned Pier, just made for the pleasure of walking over the sea. The fascination of taking in sea breezes or catching the ferry or cruise boat. I remember taking an afternoon cruise on an Isle of Man ferry as late as 1979. The boat came from Liverpool, cruised round Puffin Island and down the Menai Straits, back to Llandudno then she left for the Isle of Man. In the 1930s and 1940s you could catch a boat from or to Liverpool or the Isle of Man for the day. It is a pity somebody cannot bring this service back, I am sure that it would be popular.

A 1920s postcard showing the newly erected cenotaph in pride of place on the promenade.

After all those views of the Bay here is something different; a 1910 card showing the town hall.

Two cards that compliment each other. This advertisement card from the turn of the century shows the North Western Hotel, and the Hotel Gardens facing. Now the Crown Hotel and with a good line in lunches.

A 1930 card taken from the steps of the hotel in the previous picture. The hotel gardens are now Mostyn Street Gardens and the trees, young and just planted are still there but mature.

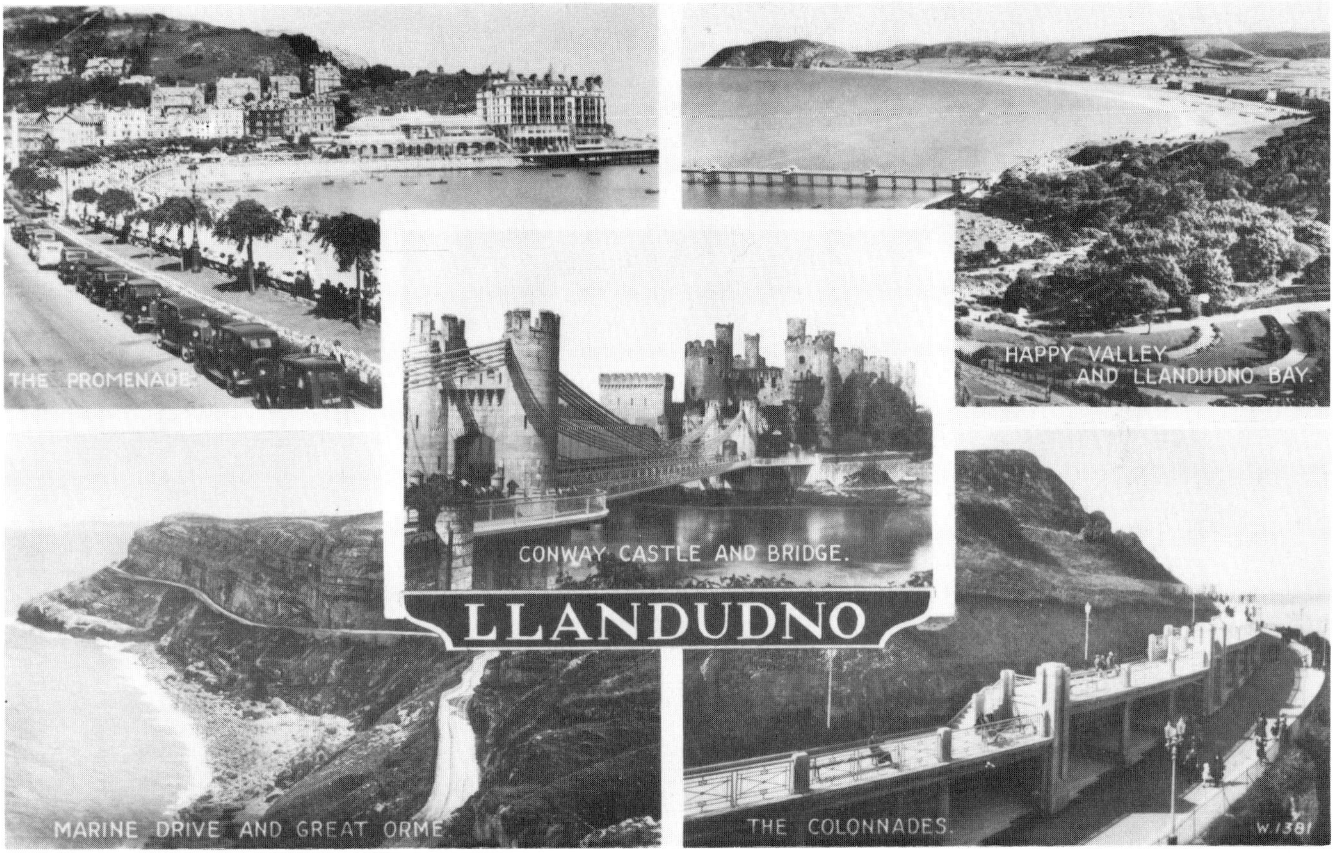

The Second World War is over and we settle down to enjoy family holidays once again as the world tries to get back to routine. A 1945 card, strangely showing Conway Castle in the middle of a Llandudno card.

LLANGOLLEN

Not just the home of the Eisteddfodd this has always been a gentle watering hole that has seen mixed fortunes over the last 120 years. The loss of the railway was a bitter blow to visitors but the well-run and exciting steam railway centre there now brings in many visitors. I have many memories and links with the town from my first cub camp at a farm near the ruined castle, my last scout camp at Vale Crucis Abbey, washing in the icy cold waters; the first Y.H.A. outing I was brave enough to undertake with two mates from Widnes, Tony Kavaner and Geoff Chambers was to Llangollen, it was such an adventure those days I felt like Livingstone going to Africa — going to Wales on a bike, and our choir outing from St. Michael's Hough Green Widnes was always to Llangollen and always lunch at the same hotel and yet we all looked surprised when the venue was announced each year. I (like everyone else on Merseyside) joined a group and Alan French, one of our group had a caravan at Vale Crucis Abbey and we had some happy days there as teenagers. So it's no surprise I will always look on the town with fond memories, it's so tied up with my growing years.

The name Llangollen comes from St. Collen who is the saint the local church is dedicated to.

A rare shot of the Chain Bridge Hotel in 1895. The bridge has been rebuilt since and the hotel has been added to more than once. Still a pleasant stop if you are in the area.

The fine bridge built in 1131 at Llangollen (referred to as ''One of the Wonders of Wales'' in a 1900 guide book) shows up as a fine, strong structure in this 1910 postcard.

The First World War is over and a holiday in Wales is once more a family treat. An almost aerial view of Llangollen printed and posted in 1919. Half way up the main street was the local cinema called the 'Dorothy' now a cafe and bookshop owned by my friend Tebor (a Welsh character) with the bookshelves where the screen was, and the books piled high where the seats were.

A card like this was produced for all the tourists' towns in England and Wales. Hard to date, as the stamp and frank are missing but I guess about 1920. The card gives the town's statistics.

RIVER & BRIDGE, LLANGOLLEN (178)

LLANGOLLEN, Denbigh (Pop. 3,000)

Wrexham 11¼ miles. *Chester 22¾ miles.*
Corwen 10¼ miles. *Early closing Thursday.*

Old market town which takes its name from the dedication of the church to St. Collen, in the charming vale of Llangollen, surrounded by majestic hills finely varied in gorse, rock and timber.

Plas Newydd was the home, from 1779 to 1830, of Lady Eleanor Butler and Miss Ponsonby, "The Ladies of Llangollen."

The famous Valle Crucis Abbey, a Cistercian foundation of 1200 is passed in a side valley on the way to the Horseshoe Pass, the summit of which is 1350 feet, then leading down into Ruthin (10 miles).

LLANGOLLEN, PLAS NEWYDD

As mentioned on the last card Plas Newydd was one of the places you had to visit in Llangollen "The Ladies of Llangollen" was the name given to Lady Eleanor Butler and Miss Sarah Ponsonby who lived here from the late 1780s until 1831. They were completely eccentric, they wore trousers, shirts and men's suits. The list of famous men who called on them in the early 19th century reads like a list in Who's Who; Browning, Tennyson, Sir Walter Scott, William Wordsworth, the Duke of Wellington and many others. It was the custom to take these ladies a personal gift and these gifts made fascinating viewing when the Hall became the property of the National Trust and was open to the public in the 1950s. This card from 1909 shows the fine black and white house.

LLANGOLLEN

We cannot leave Llangollen without returning to Valc Crucis Abbey. What is remarkable about these two cards?

The top one from 1920 and an 'Exclusive Sepiatone' and the bottom one supposedly from 1930 a 'Photocrome' card. To me it looks like the top one with the negative turned round: One of them is the wrong way round. You'll have to go and see for yourself.

PENMAENMAWR

Most people used to rush through this village after the traffic jams of pre-tunnel Conway. You would not be able to do much rushing with the width of the main street in this 1905 card. This was one of the new cards where you were allowed to write your message on the back as per the instructions printed on it.

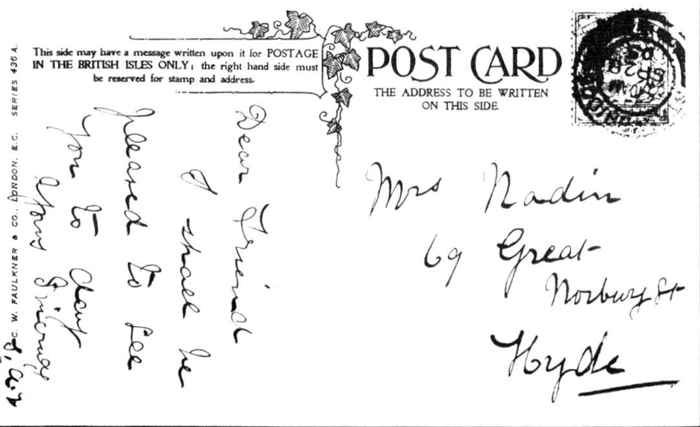

The parade and front in 1920 and fashionable ladies stroll past the bathing huts. The card was sent on Friday morning with a message to be at the station on Saturday, the next day, with the truck. Very reliable post in those days.

PEN-Y-CLIP

In 1920 when this 'Artists' card was issued the road and rail improvements at this point on the coast were considered "wonders". Now with the new Conway Tunnel this has all been revamped once more.

PENSARN

This shows Pensarn beach about 1900. The cobbles and pebbles are still there (except for the 50 in my back garden). In this same spot now is the refurbished cafe, beach shops and amusements. Well worth stopping here and watching the steam trains pass on a summer Sunday.

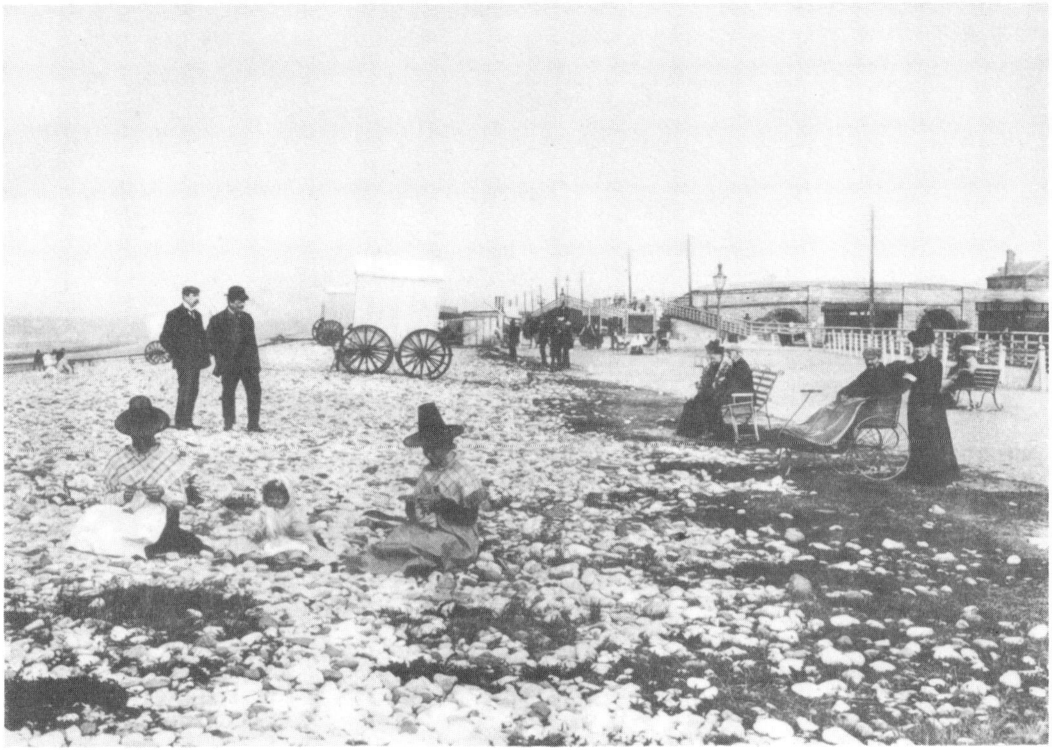

LOCAL VIEWS

If you Desire the BEST
at Popular Prices . .

ASK FOR VALENTINE'S

From the Leading Stationers Everywhere. **SERIES**

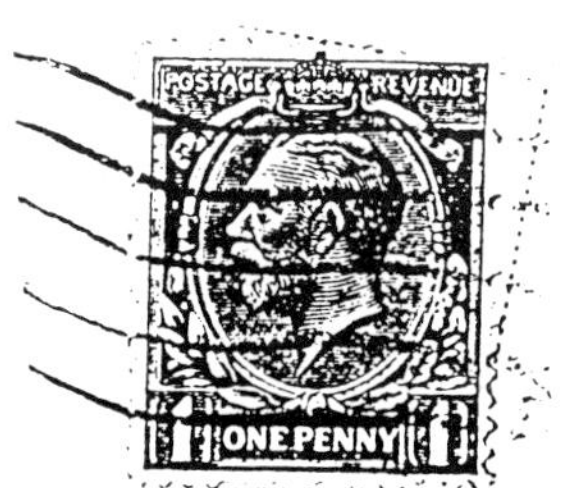

PRESTATYN

The name Prestatyn first appears on a map in 1577. Since then the town has been famed for its fresh air and glorious beaches. In Victorian days it attracted the artistic element and walkers, and many postcards from 1900 to 1914 told of the sender painting, sketching or going for sturdy walks.

A lot of the old town centre disappeared when the High Street was widened, but it is a very pleasant stroll, with good shops, and nice little cafes.

Offa's Dyke starts on the promenade at Prestatyn and there is now a monument to its start there. It was built in the 8th century by King Offa of Mercia to protect his country from marauding Welsh tribes, it runs right through Wales and ends at Chepstow. Much of its route is well marked by a long distance footpath.

If you are feeling brave and adventurous, take the top road round the town and between the Shell garage and The Cross Foxes pub, turn up the road and head up. This road climbs to 800 feet and the views from the top are marvellous — it is like flying. Don't attempt it if you have not got good brakes on your car. Walk up! In Victorian times this was referred to as 'balloon mountain' meaning it was like looking out of a balloon.

Prestatyn was the first Town in North Wales to have an outdoor bathing pool. This 1930 card praises the pool and its facilities. The open air pool has now been replaced with an indoor pool and leisure centre. It has recently been refurbished and is better than ever, after the hammering it got in the floods in 1990.

This is the lane that leads to the hill climb mentioned before. Even in 1919 it was an attractive walk.

Prestatyn boasts three beaches. Barkby, Central and Ffrith Beach. This 1920s card shows Central beach. Very different from today.

PRESTATYN

The High Street Prestatyn in the 1940s. It is still recognisable, even though there has been quite a bit of redevelopment. Note no yellow lines on the road, they hadn't been invented then.

A 1930s view from inland showing Meliden in the foreground and Prestatyn and the sea behind. Some of the open areas shown behind the town have been filled in with housing. The railway line shown clearly crossing the middle to the right of the photograph was lifted in the 1960s and now makes a very pleasant walk from Prestatyn to Dyserth.

A composite card extolling the virtues of Ffrith the most southern of Prestatyn's beaches. The council bought the area and its beach just after the First World War and developed it to attract visitors. The card was printed about 1946 and posted on August Monday 1948. This card, as were many other postcards in the 20s, 30s and 40s was written in soft pencil, and its urgent and important message has now faded.

PRESTATYN

Nant Hall Hotel, Prestatyn, shown in the early 1930s card by J.T. Burrows. This black and white building is situated on the coast road, on the right just before you reach Prestatyn. There is a story that this Hall was built by a rich land-owner for his daughter to spend her honeymoon in. When the bridegroom failed to turn up, the would be bride went and lived in the house alone. Many years later it was sold and turned into a hotel.

POST CARD

THE ADDRESS TO BE WRITTEN ON THIS SIDE.

Gertie and Harold sent this very rural view of the road out of Prestatyn, to Clara in Mayor's Road, Altrincham in July 1912. The road is now a bit wider, but still very recognisable.

RHOS-ON-SEA

Until 1954 Rhos-on-Sea had a pier. It was some 1,000 feet in length. It was built originally in Douglas, Isle of Man in 1869 and was taken from there and rebuilt at Rhos in 1896.

A late 1950s Salmon card covers most of Rhos-on-Sea. Rhos is now very popular as a retirement place (in fact I have an Uncle Bob and Auntie Marjorie firmly ensconsed there and very happily settled). But don't get the wrong idea about Rhos-on-Sea, although it still retains its air of gentility, Rhos is still very popular with the young wind-surfers and yachters of all ages, and it is a treat to walk down to the sea front and watch or take part. The beach is also idea for the family picnic.

RHOS-ON-SEA

This Valentine early colour card from the late 1950s showing Rhos Point Cafe and Shops with Old Colwyn and Colwyn Bay behind. The little shop next to the Cafe is full of interesting bric-a-brac, and postcards. It is nice on a sunny day to sit outside the cafe and enjoy a drink, or one of their delightful fish dishes. A visit is highly recommended.

Showing the Colonnade and Promenade. This was once the entrance to the Pier now turned into a sun-trap protected by glass screens. Another nice spot to sit and watch the world go by.

A mish-mash of dates on these cards but then card manufacturers could get away with it. Note the tram lines on the Whitehall Road picture. There was once a popular tram run from Llandudno to Rhos-on-Sea. There is no sign of the Pier on any of the pictures so I date them to be around the late 1950s.

POST CARD

THE ADDRESS TO BE WRITTEN ON THIS SIDE.

Shows clearly how Rhos is the southern end of the half moon shaped bay.

RHOS-ON-SEA

St. Trillo's, a 16th century chapel (only 12ft by 6ft wide) is almost on the beach. It was built by the monks from Conway Abbey and used to pray for good catches when they went fishing. At low tide you can still see the remains of a fishing weir used by the monks. Holy Communion is still said in this tiny chapel on Fridays at 8.00a.m.

LOCAL VIEWS

If you Desire the BEST

at Popular Prices . .

ASK FOR VALENTINE'S

From the Leading Stationers Everywhere. **SERIES**

RHYL (Y RHYL)

At the mouth of the river Clwyd you find sunny Rhyl. I like Rhyl, I spend quite a bit of time in Rhyl. Most summer week-ends we are in Rhyl at least once. Rhyl has the habit of shooting itself in the foot. It once had a lovely Pier, but they closed it in 1966 and left it to rot while they dithered about its future. Then they pulled it down far too fast, and they had lost their Pier. Rhyl had a lovely theatre called the Pavilion. The council thought the dome was unsafe, so the blew it up in 1974. The part that survived and was hard to demolish was the dome. The Gaiety Theatre was a pleasant theatre for smaller productions but it too went with indecent haste. The sun centre is a great asset in our inclement weather, never seems to be fully realised. Parts of Rhyl are trying very hard to improve and have lifted their image, yet 200 yards away, in other parts there are empty shops with dirty windows and peeling paint. As they used to put on the bottom of my school report — Rhyl could try harder.

A happy picture from late 1950s showing the paddling pool and behind it in great splendour is the Pavilion Theatre. 'Prince's International Circus' was the attraction 'daily at 2.30 and 7.30' boasts the banner.

RHYL

This card shows the Pier and the roller skating rink. Sadly both have now gone. The Pier was closed in 1966 and demolished in 1973. The skating rink has now gone, and a large underground car park is being built on the spot.

RHYL.

MORVILLE **Private Hotel.**

FACING Sea. Famous for its Homeliness and Excellent Cuisine. Reasonable Tariff. Garage. Under Supervision of

MRS. A. G. WALFORD, PROPRIETRESS.

'Phone and Tels., "Rhyl **100**."

An Alphabetically Arranged List of Hotels, Boarding Establishments, Schools, House and Estate Agents, at the Principal Holiday and Health Resorts, will be found at the end of this Guide.

High-Class School, Blencathra, Russell Road, Rhyl,

FOR THE DAUGHTERS OF GENTLEMEN.

Conducted by the Misses Trousdell ..

Assisted by an Efficient Staff of Resident Mistresses and Masters from Liverpool and Chester.

References kindly permitted to

His Honour, Sir HORATIO LLOYD, Judge, The Mount, Chester, and Rev. DAN EDWARDS, Vicar of Rhyl.

For further information apply to Principal.

.. Price Twopence ..

— NEW —

HANDBOOK AND GUIDE

TO

RHYL

AND ITS VICINITY.

Photo.] *THE PIER & PAVILION, RHYL.* *[Bedford.*

AND THE WALKS, DRIVES AND EXCURSIONS

IN THE NEIGHBOURHOOD.

WITH A TIME TABLE.

BY EDGAR BROOKS.

Printed and Published by ...

J. L. Allday, Shakespeare Press, Edmund St., Birmingham.

RHYL

A rare photograph from 1897 taken from the end of the 700 yard Pier. Walking this Pier was a MUST for visitors and went hand in hand with Rhyl's reputation for sunny days and healthy water.

The same year and looking at the Pier with the Grand Pavilion at its entrance. Rhyl really was an elegant place at the turn of the century. The Pavilion Theatre was built in 1890 but burnt down only 11 years later in 1901. The Amphitheatre, built to replace it, became the Gaiety Theatre. The small square monument in the middle of the promenade is a fountain, built at a cost of £150 to mark the 21st birthday of a Conway Rowley from Bodrhyddan. It was moved in 1948 into storage.

Again 1895 and the fountain dominates a wide, clean promenade. Note the crowd on the beach. I wonder if it was a prayer meeting?

A 1950s collage. The Pavilion really was a splendid building and the sun always glinted on its dome. It could be seen for miles. Many ships captains used to say that they could see the dome glistening miles out at sea, and was a landmark for them. The outdoor bathing pool and diving boards were always well used and great fun.

Something different. Ideal for church outings to send back. A 1930s card showing the interior of St. Thomas's church, Rhyl.

Moving to the late 1920s. The fountain is still there and the Gaiety Theatre now stands where the Grand Pavilion was. The White Rose omnibus in the picture, waits patiently for its passengers. White Rose ran the service from Rhyl to villages up and down the coast.

Looking down the High Street from the Railway Bridge just before World War I. The shop on the corner Wm. Roberts is still to this day a seed merchants and pet supplies.

"Y GWIR YN /|\ ERBYN Y BYD."

THE

Royal National Eisteddfod of Wales,

RHYL.

SEPTEMBER 6th, 7th, 8th, & 9th, 1892.

Rhaglen Swyddogol.

Official Programme.

Eisteddfod Frenhinol Genhedlaethol.

GORSEDD BEIRDD YNYS PRYDAIN A CHADAIR GWYNEDD.

RHYL, MEDI 6ed, 7fed, 8fed, a 9fed, 1892.

RHYL:

PUBLISHED BY TREHEARN AND AINSWORTH,

165 & 166, WELLINGTON ROAD, AND

D. TREHEARN, FINE ART DEPÔT, 61, HIGH STREET.

COPYRIGHT. PRICE 6D.

Post Card

SALMON SERIES

TRADE MARK

In 1892 the National Eisteddfod was held in Rhyl. The four day event was started on September 6th and cost over £4,000 to stage. The Eisteddfod was also held in Rhyl in 1904, 1953 and 1885. The Druids Circle can still be seen north of the Sun Centre on the Promenade.

Having a Topping Time at

RHYL

1606

A mailing novelty from the early 1930s. The horse lifts up and contains 12 small black and white photographs.

Two views of the Theatre at the beginning of the Pier, that ended life as the Gaiety. It was still called the Amphitheatre when this postcard was published in about 1908.

An earlier shot showing the interior of the Theatre. In 1980 I stood outside and looked at an advertisement for the Theatre — it looked exactly like this, and must not have changed much from opening to closing.

The south end of Rhyl was a bog, a quagmire and an eyesight. Then the river bank was strengthened the area flooded and the Marine Lake was created in 1895. The fun fair started around the turn of the century.

We leave Rhyl with this lovely painting of the Promenade and the Pavilion Theatre. A late 1930s card.

RHUDDLAN

A 1902 card showing the ivy covered castle. It must have been a very popular view, as I have found three different almost alike, just the cows kept moving. The castle was started in 1277 by Edward I. It was he who deepened the river and his ships used to berth by the square tower in the right of the card. There was once a lot of traffic between here and the Isle of Man. If you go up the High Street in Rhuddlan make a point of looking for the old Parliament House. Edward I held his first parliament in that building in 1283.

ST. ASAPH (LLANELWY)

A lovely of the Cathedral at St. Asaph taken before 1900. This, the smallest Cathedral in Britain, was founded by the primate of Scotland, St. Mungo (sometimes called St. Kentigern) in the 6th century, after he was forced to leave Scotland due to persecution. Later, he returned north leaving a local holy man Asa, later named St. Asaph in charge and the city took his name. St. Asaph is the second smallest city in the British Isles. The Cathedral has been sacked and rebuilt quite a few times. The present building was started in 1482 and was restored in the 19th century. It has a fascinating collection of bible and artifacts, and is well worth a visit.

ST ASAPH

A 1915 postcard showing the bridge and Cathedral tower dominating the city. The memorial in the Cathedral is dedicated to the first ever translation of the bible into Welsh.

TOWYN (TWYN)

TWN.180. CLOCK TOWER AND CHURCH. TOWYN. Copyright Frith Ltd.

Can you recognise the peaceful street and church in this 1940s card of a gentler age?

An Awkward Mistake

A young man from Wales being engaged to a Young Lady, and being desirous of buying her something for a Birthday Present, and not being able to decide himself, went shopping with his sister. Entering a Draper's Shop she purchased a pair of Knickers and he a pair of gloves for his Lady Love. A little error occurred in sending the parcels off, with the result that the Knickers were sent to the Young Lady instead of the Gloves, with the following letter:—

My Dear Jessie,

I do hope you will accept this little token instead of a silly Birthday Card. Oh! how I wish no other hands would touch them after you have put them on. I know dearest, that such a wish is in vain, a thousand young men may touch them, and other eyes than mine may see them on you. I bought the smallest size I could get, and if they are too large let them wrinkle down a bit. Always wear them when we are together, as I want to see how they fit you. My sister says she has to clean hers very often, as so many young men soil them with their hands, but you can clean them with benzine if you leave them on to dry. I do hope, Dear, they are not too small, and be careful Dear, not to wet them, and be sure to blow into them before you put them on.

Yours, with love,

PERCY

An unusual card from 1900 and very risque at the time. Probably printed abroad or by some local printer. No stamp on the reverse yet a message, so it probably went inside an envelope. The early smutty postcard.

A good example of a romantic card posted about 1910 from North Wales to a young lady in Belfast, again probably in an envelope due to the amorous message from the writer on the back.

THE ANCHOR'S WEIGHED.

The tear fell gently from her eye,
When last we parted on the shore;
Her bosom heaved with many a sigh
To think I ne'er might see her more.
"Dear youth," she cried, "and can'st thou haste away,
My heart will break; a little moment stay,
Alas, I cannot, I cannot part from thee!"
"The anchor's weighed! the anchor's weighed!
Farewell! farewell! remember me!"

245

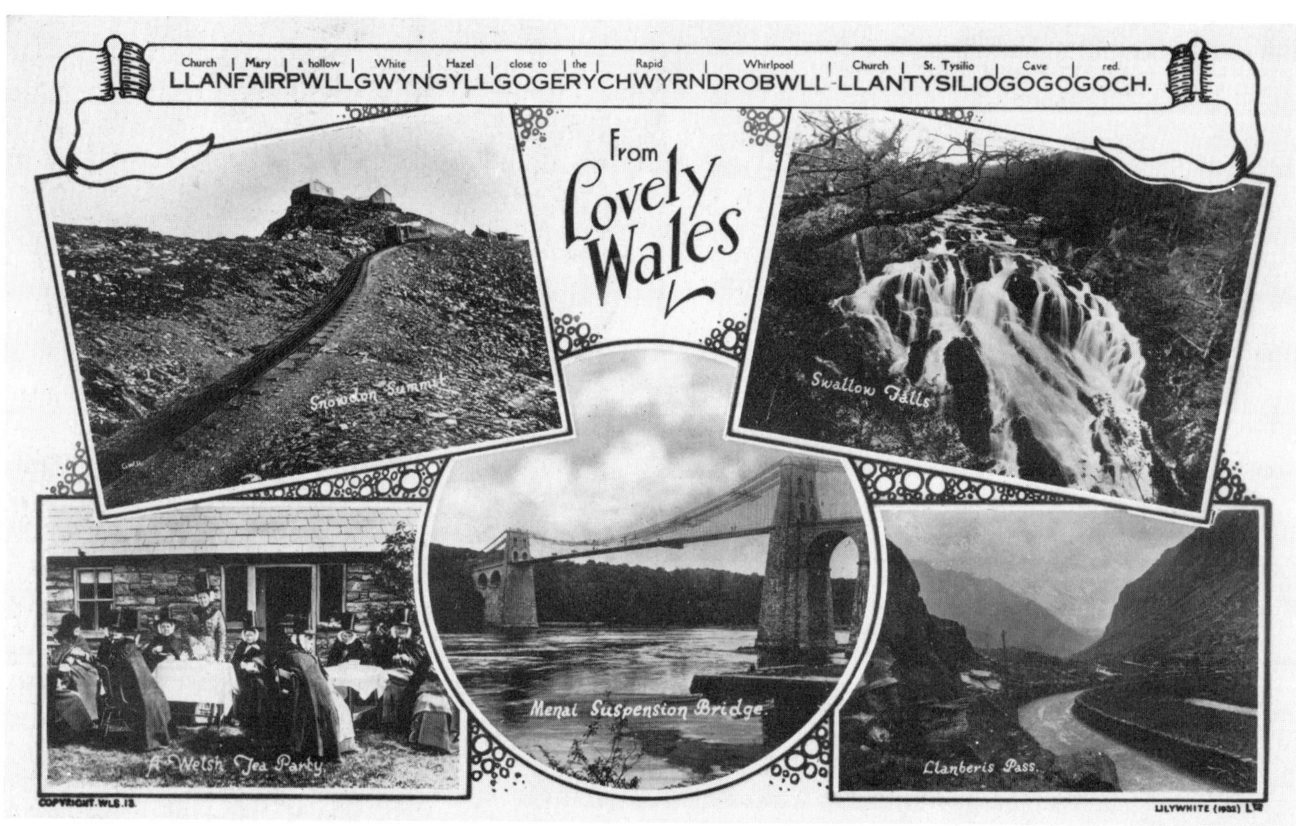

Another composite card again using the Llanfairgogogoch name to push the card. This is one of Lilywhite's and the earliest I can find with Welsh instructions printed on the back.

A very clever postcard. Posted in Llandudno in September 1913. This Glazette Greeting card informed Miss H. Luish in Batley that her friend Nellie had been all over Anglesey and seen the Swallow Falls and the Fairy Glen. MY! people were busy then, if a holiday maker hadn't been on at least 4 trips, or visits it was considered a lazy holiday.

CONWAY CASTLE.
PROMENADE FROM GREAT ORME
LLANDUDNO.
LEDR BRIDGE,
BETTWS-Y-COED.
PIER FROM HAPPY VALLEY
LLANDUDNO.
THE FRONT, LLANDUDNO.
LLANDUDNO
40

THE WELSH LANGUAGE

Here is a list of the more common Welsh words found in place names:

Aber	a river mouth
Afon	a river
Allt	a hillside
Bach or Fach	little, small
Bedd	a grave
Blaen	head of a valley
Bod	to be
Bron/Fron	a hillside
Bryn	a hill
Bwlch	a pass
Caer	a fort or walled town
Carn/Carnedd	a cairn or heap of stones
Cefn	a ridge
Clogwyn	a precipice
Clwyd	a gate
Coch/Goch	red
Coed	a wood
Croes/Groes	a cross
Cwm	the valley of a stream
Din, Dinas	a fort
Drws	a gate or pass
Du, Dulas	black, dark
Dwy	water
Dyffryn	the valley of a river
Egllwys	a church
Fechan	little, small
Ffynnon	a spring or well
Gelli	a grove
Glan	a bank or shore
Glyn	a glen
Gwyn/Wyn/Wen	white
Hen	old
Isaf	lowest
Llan	a church, parish or village
Llyn	a lake
Llys	a court, or place
Mach	a secure place
Maen/Faen	a stone
Maes/Faes	a field
Mawr/Fawr	great, large
Moel/Foel	a rounded, bare hill
Morfa	a marsh
Mynach	a monk
Mynydd/Fyndd	a mountain
Nant	a stream
Neigr	black, dark
Newydd	new
Pant	a hollow
Pen/Ben	a head or summit
Plas	a hall or mansion
Pont/Bont	a bridge
Porth	a gate or opening
Pwll	a pool or ditch
Rhiw	a hill
Rhos	a moor
Rhudd	red, crimson
Rhydd	a ford
Sarn	a causway
Tir	earth or land
Traeth	a beach
Tre, Tref/Dre, Dref	a town
Twr	a tower
Ty	a house
Tywod	sand
Tywyn	sea-shore
Uchaf	highest
Waun	a moor
Y, Yr	the, of or on the
Yn	in, at
Ynys	an island
Ystrad	vale or valley (or a river)

NORTHERN CLASSIC REPRINTS

The Manchester Man

(Mrs. G. Linnaeus Banks)

Re-printed from an 1896 illustrated edition — undoubtedly the finest limp-bound edition ever. Fascinating reading, includes Peterloo. Over 400 pages, wonderfully illustrated.

ISBN 1 872226 16 7 £4.95

The Manchester Rebels

(W Harrison Ainsworth)

A heady mixture of fact and fiction combined in a compelling story of the Jacobean fight for the throne of England. Manchester's involvement and the formation of the Manchester Regiment. Authentic illustrations.

ISBN 1 872226 29 9 £4.95

Hobson's Choice (the Novel)

(Harold Brighouse)

The humorous and classic moving story of Salford's favourite tale. Well worth re-discovering this enjoyable story. Illustrated edition. Not been available since 1917, never before in paperback.

ISBN 1 872226 36 1 £4.95

NORTHERN CLASSIC REPRINTS

Poems & Songs Of Lancashire

(Edwin Waugh)

A wonderful quality reprint of a classic book by undoubtedly one of Lancashire's finest poets. First published 1859 faithfully reproduced. Easy and pleasant reading, a piece of history.

ISBN 1 872226 27 2 £4.95

The Dock Road

(J. Francis Hall RN)

A seafaring tale of old Liverpool. Set in the 1860s, with the American Civil War raging and the cotton famine gripping Lancashire. Period illustrations.

ISBN 1 872226 37 X £4.95

The Lancashire Witches

(W. Harrison Ainsworth)

A beautifully illustrated edition of the most famous romance of the supernatural.

ISBN 1 872226 55 8 £4.95

OTHER BOOKS IN THIS SERIES

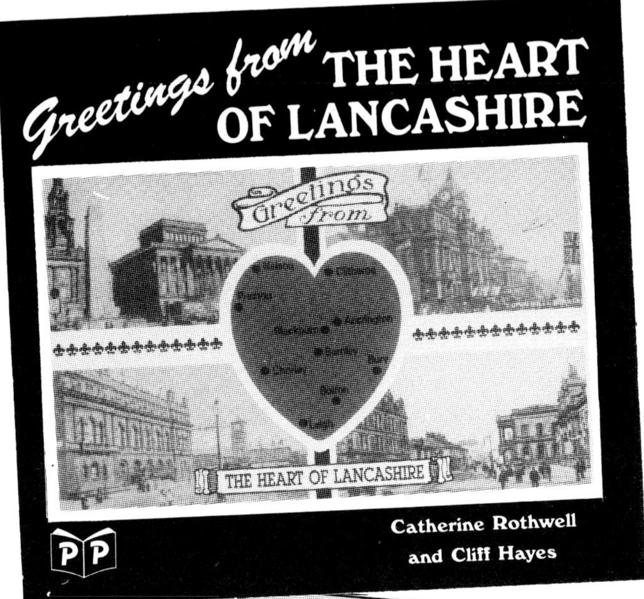